Two Big Feelings

Angry and Sad

My cousin's birthday is today!
We're going to the store to buy her a
present. Before we go, Daddy invites
me to have a heart-to-heart. That's
a special kind of talk.

"Ammar," Daddy says, "we have a job to do today."

"We're buying a birthday cake and a present for Adrias," I say.

"Right," Daddy says. "There are a lot of fun things at the store, aren't there? A lot of fun things we might want for ourselves."

"Yes," I agree. I love going to the store.

"I might really want a treat," says Daddy. "What if I say 'please, Ammar, oh PLEASE may I have some smoked almonds? They're my very favorite.'"

I giggle. Daddy is so funny.

"No, Daddy, no almonds today."

"What if there's something YOU really want?" says Daddy. "Like a big, shiny butterfly balloon on a string?"

"I'll have to say 'not today.'"

"Because it's Adrias's turn," I say.

"That's right, Habibi," says Daddy.

Habibi means "my love" in Arabic,
one of the languages we speak in
my family.

We go to the bakery first so we can pick out Adrias's birthday cake. I love to look at all of the cakes and treats.

"I want chocolate for my birthday cake," I tell Daddy.

He smiles. "Which one should we get for Adrias?" I pick the chocolate one with candy on top!

"That's a good one," says Daddy. "Now let's go see if we can find a present."

We walk over to where the toys are, and I see the perfect thing even before we get there: a sloth wearing a hat.

"This!" I say. I pick it up and give it a big hug.

"That's a wonderful idea, Ammar; you're such a thoughtful gift giver."

I pick up a smaller sloth with a hat on.
"And one for me?" I ask.

"Let's put that one back, Ammar.
It's Adrias's turn today. Shall we go
to the checkout spot and pay for her
cake and present?"

I give the little sloth one more hug
and put it back on the shelf.

"Yes," I say.

When we get to the checkout spot, we have to wait our turn.

There's a shelf full of animal toys right next to me, and I see a lion. Lions are my favorite kind of animal.

"Daddy, look! It's a lion!"

"I see that, Ammar. That's a fun thing to look at."

"And take it home?" I ask.

"It's a wonderful lion, but we're not going to buy it today," says Daddy.

"I want a lion," I say, and I sit down on the floor.

"Ammar, remember? It's Adrias's turn today."

"I want it. I want the lion!" I'm hot and my jacket feels too tight. I throw it on the floor. "My turn!"

"Ammar," Daddy says.

I cry really hard for a long time.
Daddy is right next to me but he
sounds far away.

"Ammar, I'm here with you."

"I'm going to pick you up and carry you outside," Daddy says.

He picks me up and we leave the cake and Adrias's stuffed animal with the checkout person.

"We'll come back for that in a little while," he says, and carries me out of the store.

I rest my head on Daddy's shoulder
and just cry and cry. I am so sad.

We didn't get a lion
OR a cake
OR a sloth with a hat on.

My face hurts from being full of tears,
and I feel like my tummy is missing.

"Oh Habibi, this has been so hard for you," Daddy says. "You were angry and sad today. Two big feelings together is a lot, isn't it? Let's have a bosa," and he kisses me.

I cry for a little while, and then I'm ready to go back inside.

Daddy lets me put his card in the machine to pay, and I carry the sloth with the hat on out of the store.

Daddy carries the cake.

When we get back to our car, Daddy says, "Ammar, driving to Adrias's house will take a little while. Would a short sleep feel nice on the way?"

I shake my head—I don't want to sleep—but my eyes close, and when I'm ready to open them again, we're at Adrias's house.

I'm ready for the party.

We go inside and I give Adrias her present. She smiles and hugs it.

"Thank you, Ammar. I love it! The hat is my favorite part. Let's go have some cake."

Can you find a page where Ammar felt angry?

Can you make an angry face?

When have you felt angry?